for my father

STAN VAN STEENDAM

READING THE STREETS
FADING CITY TYPOGRAPHY

TEXT BY ANDREU BALIUS

LUSTER

Burgstraat, Ghent

A JOURNEY THROUGH THE ALPHABET

Our Latin alphabet, which has more than 2,000 years of history, continues to offer an endless variety of forms in its thousands of possible combinations. We are accustomed to reading it in its many written manifestations, in newspapers, books, magazines and on web pages... but we rarely pay attention to other, less conventional forms of reading which are also expressed through letters.

    Letters, the symbols used in the signs that inundate the streets of our cities, are also a "literary" form, a way of understanding the place where we live. Through words, texts, and above all through letters and the evocative, expressive power of their forms, we can learn about the techniques, values and aesthetic tastes that have prevailed in different eras.

Letters, formed in the multitude of styles used in commercial signs, are graphic symbols which "print" the streets, converting them into the pages of a book through which we can read the city, subjectively and creatively.

In the 1960s, the situationists wandered the streets of Paris seeking out new everyday experiences. From a "situationist" point of view, the city can be understood as a space for experimentation in which the *dérive* (drift), a journey without a fixed route, can be transformed into a new form of urban narrative.

The city and its letters offer different routes that are distinct from any conventional tourist route, like a game in which you learn and re-learn a space through its graphic signs. This is a new "psychogeography" of space based on graphic elements, reconstructing a map of our daily surroundings - our avenues, streets and squares - based on signs and letters, the phonetic symbols that make the urban landscape legible through written language.

Andreu Balius, type designer

Rua dos Cavaleiros, Lisbon

Boulevard Poissonnière, Paris

15   Rua de O Século, Lisbon

17 Covenant Close, Edinburgh

18 Plaça del Pedró, Barcelona

Boulevard de Bonne Nouvelle, Paris

21 Rue de l' Avenir - Toekomststraat, Brussels

25 Rue du Choeur - Koorstraat, Brussels

26   Bristo Port, Edinburgh

Rue Berckmansstraat, Brussels

28 George IV Bridge, Edinburgh

Boulevard de Sébastopol, Paris

35   Rue Ernest Allardstraat, Brussels

Carrer de la Junta de Comerç, Barcelona

41 Spuistraat, Amsterdam

45 Berka Joselewicza, Krakow

46 Ganzendries, Ghent

Nicolson Square, Edinburgh

53 Bolesława Prusa, Warsaw

Plaça de Tetuan, Barcelona

Rue des Martyrs, Paris

57 Rua das Portas de Santo Antão, Lisbon

Aleje Jerozolimskie, Warsaw

61 Praça da Alegria, Lisbon

Rua João das Regras, Lisbon

65 Rua João das Regras, Lisbon

68 Rua dos Fanqueiros, Lisbon

69 Rua Santo António dos Capuchos, Lisbon

71 Świętokrzyska, Warsaw

Rue Haute - Hoogstraat, Brussels

Avenida Almirante Reis, Lisbon

75 Rua dos Fanqueiros, Lisbon

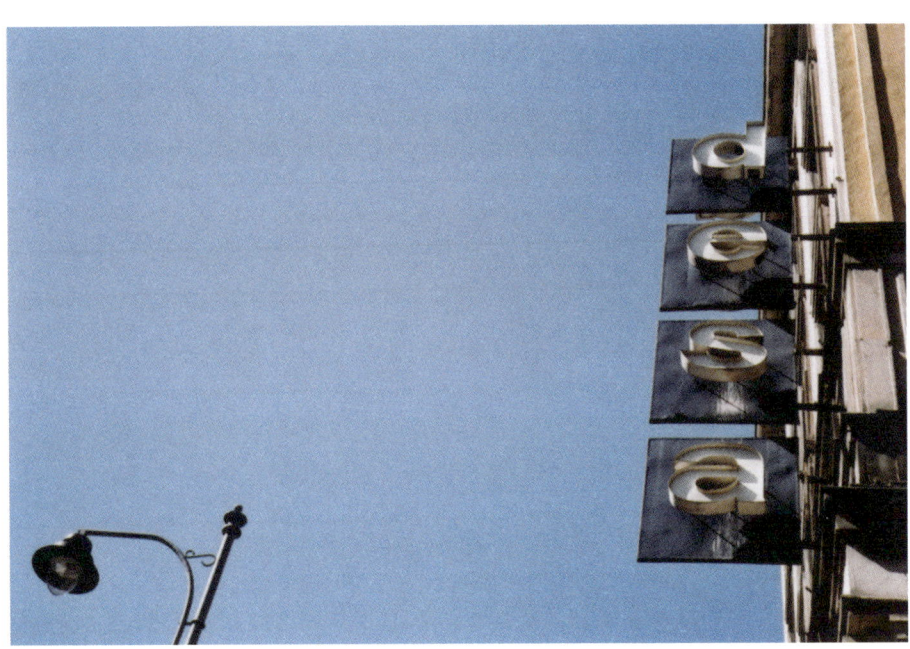

80   Marszałkowska, Warsaw

85   Rua do Jardim do Regedor, Lisbon

89   Carrer de Balmes, Barcelona

Rua da Rosa, Lisbon

Boulevard de Sébastopol, Paris

97 Gran Via de les Corts Catalanes, Barcelona

Rua Jacinta Marto, Lisbon

101 Rue de l'Argonne - Argonnestraat, Brussels

105 Binnenkant, Amsterdam

107 Boulevard Ornano, Paris

Rua dom Luís I, Lisbon

113 Prins Hendrikkade, Amsterdam

Boulevard Poissonnière, Paris

COMMERCIAL SIGNS AS FRAGMENTS
OF AN URBAN POEM

The city - any city - consists of streets, blocks, passageways, squares and avenues, parks, gardens, alleys and corners, all waiting to be discovered... A city is "tasted" step by step, gazing as you stroll, scanning every corner, sniffing the air that envelops the buildings and the aromas that emerge from their windows (even if these are sometimes unpleasant). At this level of exploration, we can read the city from a different perspective, a dimension that goes far beyond the conventional reading given to us by the standard travel guides and tourist routes.

The commercial sign, as an element that identifies a place, has always been a way of personalising a business and the activity that takes place there.

There were shop signs in ancient Pompeii and throughout the medieval period. But it was not until after the industrial revolution that commercial signs took on a greater role in an economic framework of increased competitiveness in modern cities.

Signage has its basis in calligraphy and lettering, although it was influenced by printing and reproduction techniques, and by the typefaces used for commercial posters which proliferated from the mid-19th century onwards.

A signboard is more than just decoration for a shop, though it is usually located on the external façade of the building, interacting with the architecture. Architecture and commercial signs, together with the type of material used (stone, wood, wrought iron, mosaic, tiles) often go hand in hand. Some signs do not match the architecture as well as others, but we cannot separate one from the other when we consider that the sign is the visible, external part of a business. A signboard is a "call" which informs, indicates and "attracts" the city dweller. In turn, it also signals the identity of a shop or business.

Signs "compete" with each other, in their showiness, magnitude and originality... regardless of the type of business they are advertising. But although commercial signs match the specific aesthetic design of the business they identify - which in most cases they must do - this does not lessen the effect of the sign on the urban environment, on the context in which it exists.

Like architecture, signs correspond to a specific moment in history, and although more ephemeral in nature than architecture, they reflect the cultural and aesthetic values of a given moment in time or historical period.

These recurring signs which accumulate across the urban fabric of the city represent an amalgam of visual suggestions, catching the eye and inspiring the curious wanderer.

Rue de la Chapelle, Paris

121 Korte Koepoortstraat, Antwerp

123 Avenue Brillat-Savarinlaan, Brussels

125 Rue Sneessensstraat, Brussels

126 Rua das Portas de Santo Antão, Lisbon

127 Carrer de Girona, Barcelona

129 Rua da Boavista, Lisbon

Carrer de Provença, Barcelona

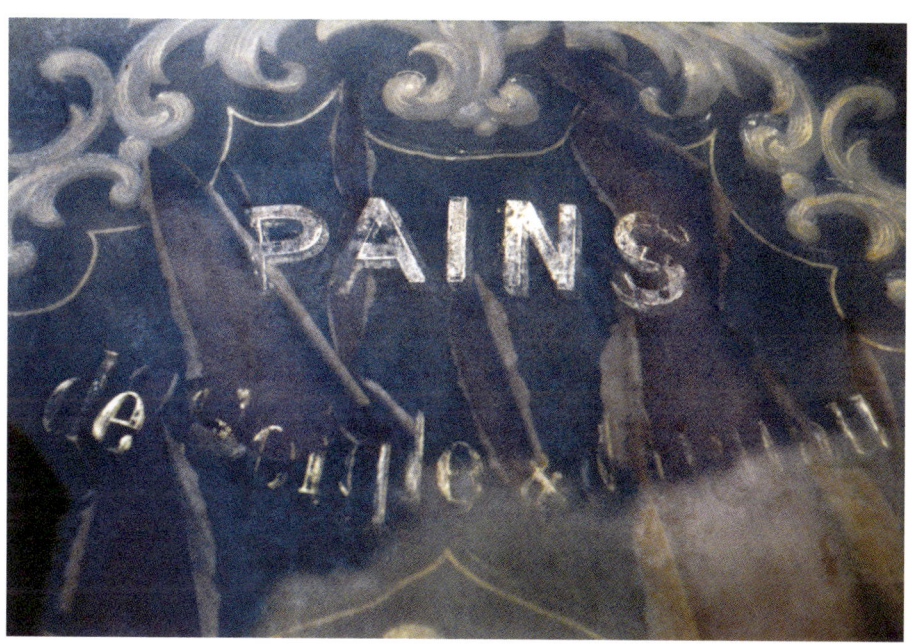

133   Rue Duhesme, Paris

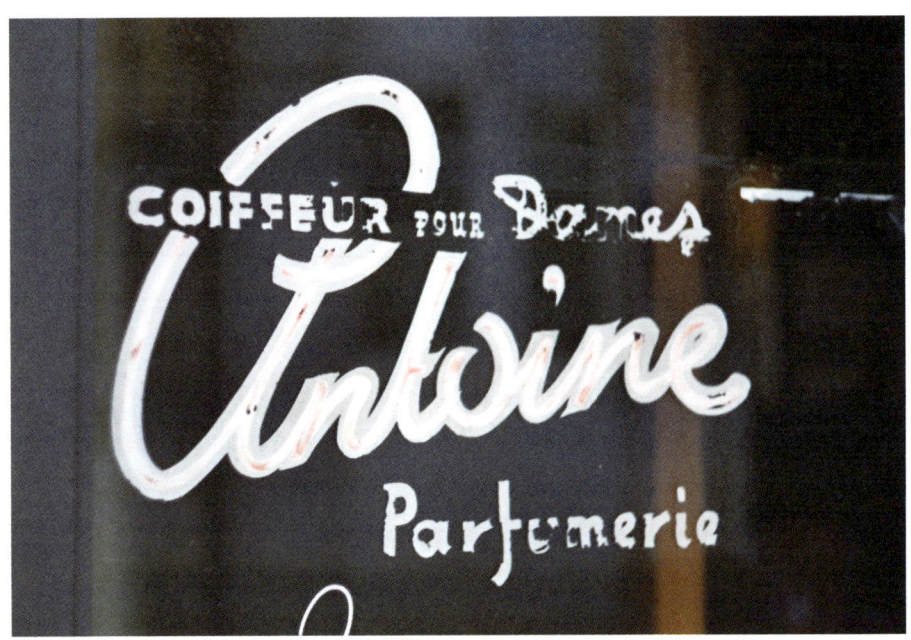

Lange Nieuwstraat, Antwerp

137   Rue de Turbigo, Paris

Rue des Moucherons - Muggenstraat, Brussels

Rue Duhesme, Paris

145 Rambla de Sant Josep, Barcelona

Rue Catinat, Paris

Rua Áurea, Lisbon

149 Rue de Turbigo, Paris

151 Rua dos Condes de Monsanto, Lisbon

Kazimierza Brodzińskiego, Krakow

153　Jana Zamoyskiego, Krakow

155 Carrer Ample, Barcelona

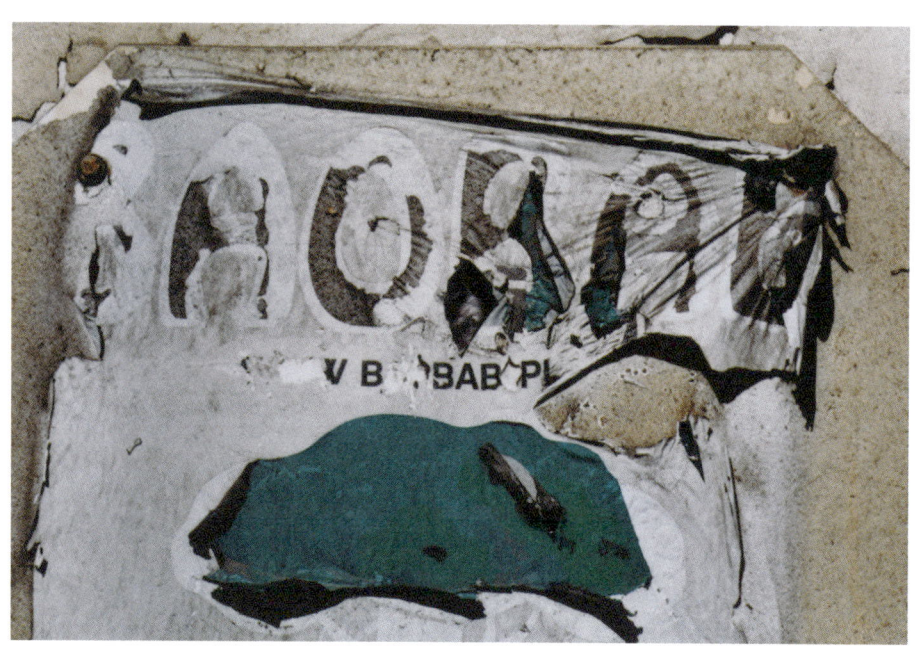

157 Calçada do Carmo, Lisbon

159 Rue des Floristes - Bloemistenstraat, Brussels

161 Rua do Arsenal, Lisbon

165 Avenue Michelet, Paris

167 Carrer de Trafalgar, Barcelona

169 Rue du Lavoir - Wasserijstraat, Brussels

171 Passage Jouffroy, Paris

175 Carrer dels Boters, Barcelona

176 Bożego Ciała, Krakow

Carrer de Guifré, Barcelona

Warrender Park Road, Edinburgh

181 Rue Saint-Denis, Paris

185 Holyrood Road, Edinburgh

187 Rua de São Nicolau, Lisbon

188 Rambla de Sant Josep, Barcelona

189 Carrer d'en Xuclà, Barcelona

191 Ronda de Sant Pere, Barcelona

193 Carrer del Carme, Barcelona

195 Szpitalna, Krakow

197 Rua da Boavista, Lisbon

199 Oudezijds Kolk, Amsterdam

201　Leidseplein, Amsterdam

203 Rua da Madalena, Lisbon

205 Magere Brug, Amsterdam

THANKS:
Tania and Dettie for your assistance and support, Andreu for being part of this journey, the whole Luster team and the people who gave me a lot of energy while making this book: Alicia, Anna, Dries, Joke, Jolein, Josep, José and Rasa.

READING THE STREETS
Fading City Typography

Photography & Typographic Design: Stan Van Steendam
Text: Andreu Balius

D/2015/12.005/11
ISBN 978 94 6058 1496
NUR 656
© 2015 Luster, Antwerp
www.lusterweb.com
Printed in Belgium

photo page 4-5: Rue Pierre Haret, Paris
photo page 206-207: Rue de la Clé - Sleutelstraat, Brussels

All rights reserved.
No part of this publication may be reproduced, stored in a retrieval system, or transmitted, in any form or by any means, without the prior written consent of the publisher. An exception is made for short excerpts which may be cited for the sole purpose of reviews.